The Movement of Bodies

For Brian Smith
Chief Archivist, Shetland

The Movement of Bodies
Sheenagh Pugh

seren

Seren is the book imprint of
Poetry Wales Press Ltd
Nolton Street, Bridgend, Wales, CF31 3BN
www.seren-books.com

ISBN 1-85411-376-3

A CIP record for this title is available from the British Library.

The publisher acknowledges the financial assistance
of the Welsh Books Council.

Printed by Bell & Bain Ltd, Glasgow

Cover photograph: Jonathan Browning

Contents

Times Like Places	7
Blue Plaque and Memorial Bench	8
Comfort	9
The Movement of Bodies	10
The Gold Sky of Venus	12
Forgiven	13
Catnip	15
Gate	16
The Navigator Loses the Sea	18
Chocolate from the Famine Museum	19
Stalemate	21
The Curator and the Art of Concealment	22
The Fuchsia	24
The Bereavement of the Lion-Keeper	26
Golden Rabbits	27
The Windfarm Angels	28
Pride	29
Baliasta Kirkyard	31
Best Jesus in Show	33
The Grave of the Grande Armée at Vilnius	35
Adzio's Story	38
The Anderson Graveyard, Aith	40
The Man On His Back	42
Fiction	43
Googlisms:	45
1.The Sonnet	45
2.The Poet	46
3.The Reader	47
The Street of Small Houses	48
Generosity	50
Buying Vinyl	51
In Love Without	53
The Thief of Love	54
Love Is	55

Ballad of the Lovesick Traveller   57
Murderers Grow Old   58
The Garden of the Last Nizam   59
The Ex-Poet Writes HTML   60
Flying Into Sunset   61
Place Names   62
Nicola's Tree   64
Learning Hindi   65
The Curious Drawer   66
  1. The Ermine   66
  2. Young Man Among Roses   67
  3. Sidney's Sister   69
  4. Henry Percy, 9th Earl of Northumberland 70
  5. Unknown Young Man Against   71
     a Background of Flames

Acknowledgements   72

Times Like Places

There are times like places: there is weather
the shape of moments. Dark afternoons
by a fire are Craster in the rain
and a pub they happened on, unlooked-for
and welcoming, while a North Sea gale
spat spume at the rattling windows.

And most August middays can take him
to the village in Sachsen-Anhalt,
its windows shuttered against the sun,
and a hen sleeping in the dusty road,
the day they picked cherries in a garden
so quiet, they could hear each other breathe.

Nor can he ever be on a ferry,
looking back at a boat's wake, and not think
of the still, glassy morning off the Hook,
when it dawned on him they didn't talk
in sentences any more: didn't need to,
each knowing what the other would say.

The worst was Aberdeen, when they walked
the length of Union Street not speaking,
choking up, glancing sideways at each other,
but never at the same time. Black cats
and windy bridges bring it all back,
eyes stinging. Yet even this memory

is dear to him, now that no place or weather
or time of day can happen to them both.
On clear winter nights, he scans the sky
for Orion's three-starred belt, remembering
whose arms warmed him, the cold night
he first saw it; who told him its name.

Blue Plaque and Memorial Bench

i.m. George Mackay Brown

Every year, if I can, I'll walk down
that street, as far as the flat

that was yours. I'll read the blue plaque
on the wall, telling how long

you lived there, how long you were happy
to have no more of the world

than this. And then I'll walk on
a little way, to the bench

they have named for you. It looks over
the harbour mouth, where the ships

come and go, where Franklin sailed out
into myth, where the men from the north

first entered this place and possessed it
by naming it. Here where you sat

and watched the whole world, living
and dead, come in on the tide.

Comfort

John Thomson, d. 1618

You would have to know where he lived,
how his croft clung to a hillside
forty times its size, on sufferance.

To stand under meteor showers
and northern lights, under a sky so vast
it swallowed his voice,

to see daily the breathtaking sweep
of hills, green and purple breakers
of surging stone,

to hear the ravishing inhuman voices
of birds, water, wind. You would need
to look out from his land,

where the ocean glitters beyond what eyes
can bear, the view he shared with no-one,
to understand John Thomson,

who, long ago, was strangled for seeking
the stable's warmth and, with soft words
of comfort, making love to his mare.

The Movement of Bodies

He fractured white light into seven colours,
reckoned the distance to the moon,

wrote laws for the movement
of bodies: no mystery to him,

until now. Planets in their orbit,
the sea's tides, his eyes

locked to the lit face
of the young mathematician.

A body at rest remains so
unless some force act on it.

So many years, no joy
but in numbers, no troubling

of the flesh. The pink tongue-tip
idly licking a finger

constricts his heart. His edges
flicker, scintillate, like a heat-haze.

A hand brushes his cheek
and it colours: *to each action*

an equal and opposite reaction.
He tries to think straight:

the moon. I worked out its mass. Moonlight,
kissing in moonlight. The movement

of bodies. The moon draws
the tides. A knife in my eye.

Once, probing for truth,
he nearly blinded himself.

This time, he will flinch
from the lacerating light.

Legend will say he died a virgin
and never saw the sea.

The Gold Sky of Venus

When he was eight and book-mad, they took him
for the first time to a high building
full of books, furnished floor to ceiling
with shelves of songs, stories, answers, dreams,

and they said "choose", and he burst out crying,
because he knew that even in a lifetime
he'd never get to read all of them.
He can smile about it now. It's something

you get used to. What were once destinations
– Samarkand, Shanghai, Saqqara –
have become the places he never saw,
a slight ache in the imagination.

But tonight he watched a programme about Venus,
where sun never pierces the dense cloud
but glows behind it, turning it to gold,
and tonight the ache is worse, the sense of loss

and waste and unread books, and his life
that seems to him worth nothing if he must die
and never see the beaten-gold sky
of Venus, bearing down like pure grief.

Forgiven

Bad boy, going on fifty, trace the bones
through your skin; you're like some consumptive

from old times. Your starry eyes,
your paper face. And it's still a child's,

was always a child's face. Lit
with brilliance. *Jesus, I'm good at this,*

I'm fucking great. Cursing and spitting,
then crumpling afterwards. You didn't mean it,

nor the drunken threats, the head-butts;
you were baffled as any child

by adult anger. *But I said sorry.*
And it didn't make things all right.

Wives walked away; you cried their names
in the night. TV sets crashed

through first-floor windows: you too, once.
A sarky plod sneered, "No real damage,

luckily he landed on his head".
But I remember you winning a match

on crutches, hopping round the table,
looking sick with pain. And I remember

days you couldn't hit a ball wrong,
you with your hopeless stance, your head

jerking on the shot, your shining
bloody genius. Hey there,

you with the stars in your eyes,
the cancer burrowing and nesting

in your throat. Your ghost-voice,
still bruised, still plaintive: *why me?*

All your life, people have softened
to that child's wail, fed you

more vodka, more nicotine, more tabs,
because the joy of talent demands

forgiveness. Wrecked you, it did,
and now, what can anyone say

to a hurt that can't be made better
but *it's all right, you're forgiven*?

Catnip

Deep inside, licking the pale-spiked bush,
stroking his tongue along the serrated edges

of minty leaves, setting free the scent
and rolling in it, over and over, breathing it

until his whole world is this piercing note
he can hardly hold, a psychosexual high

that sends him skittering, pawing at air,
glassy-eyed, mewing, breathing hard

and fast, till he falls asleep, complete
and exhausted. Hundreds of years ago,

so they say, hangmen chewed this root
before the job, before the careful positioning

of their man, before the sudden jerk
arched his body, before he collapsed limp.

You, my small mutated tiger, chew leaves
for fun only. When you want to kill,

you do it cold sober; you don't ask
the sparrow's forgiveness, and you don't pray.

Gate

Years later
he would tell how, strolling
through formal gardens,

he stopped dead.
Across the lawn, a black
wrought-iron framework,

and, curling,
flowing, insinuating
round its straight lines,

a gold filigree
of tendrils, vine-leaves. *So bright,*
he'd always murmur,

so glittering.
The gilt scraps poised
on that airy skeleton

as if, any moment,
they might flutter down.
It was autumn

fixed in metal,
glinting instants, evanescent
and captured,

iron laughter,
locked joy, quavers
on a black stave.

The whole thing sang,
he'd say. He had forgotten
long ago

what time of year
it was in the garden,
what flowers grew there,

and whatever lay
beyond the gate, it never
seemed to matter

The Navigator Loses the Sea

William Dampier, 1652-1715

Thirty years ago, he wrote the book
of these seas: two hundred years later,

they'll still be using it. Now he sails
as pilot to Woodes Rogers, back on the roads

and channels he once charted, an old man
looking out from the rail, and nothing he sees

is at all familiar. He can't find
the safe route to Juan Fernandez;

he's misplaced the Galapagos. They ask
about Butung. *No, I was never there.*

Later, below, he finds it in his book;
he spends a lot of time learning the names

and places that have slipped from his mind,
hoping to bluff the captain a bit longer.

A navigator who has lost the sea.
In the Cape Verdes, he reads of salt pans,

vast and silver, and his own excitement
at the great birds, more than he could count,

wherever he looked. *"They were like a wall
of new red brick."* He stares at the word,

its arbitrary, meaningless letters,
wondering what flamingos look like.

Chocolate from the Famine Museum

Strokestown, Co. Roscommon

Reading numbers on a wall,
so many thousand evicted,
exiled, starved,

soon palls. The boys are looking
for buttons to press,
and Sir's at a loss

how to bring it alive. He tries
to give them the reek
of peat smoke and lamp oil

in a cramped turf cabin,
wishing there was a replica
they could crowd into.

At every turn, language
fails him. *Starving*
means wanting dinner,

not boiling boot-leather
till you can chew it,
hoping it stays down.

They sailed to America,
he laments, to lads
who've flown there

on holiday, who make nothing
of oceans. They fidget
through the video,

dying for their reward:
the gift shop.
Their faces light up,

for the first time, at sheep
in green hats, penny whistles,
toy blackthorn sticks,

and the chocolate. Praline,
ganache, mint, mocha, truffle.
They're spoiled for choice,

their day flavoured
for ever with the velvet
dark in their mouths.

Stalemate

Karl Schlechter, 1874-1918

I want to stroll with Karl Schlechter
in nineteen-hundred, down a street of stone

the sun's turned to honey. From some window
a piano's playing slow, and Karl's sad eyes

kindle a little. I ask about his chess,
why he always offers a draw,

and he shrugs. White pigeons gurr
on the sills. "I hate that look in men's eyes

when they lose." I love him. We buy cherries
from a stall, morellos, dark, half-bitter,

and feed them to each other. I kiss him,
tasting them in his mouth. I want to tell him

"Karl, you die starving, at forty-four,
and you could be world champion. Play to win."

But then he wouldn't be who he is,
and I wouldn't come all the way

from the next century to hold hands
with the drawing master, watching

the light slant, hearing pigeons hush,
one by one, into sleep. Gentleman; gentle man.

The Curator and the Art of Concealment

See this one. Just another landscape,
you'd say, a stony meadow? But watch:
if I sponge just *here*, very gently,
... can you see the goat? And here, and here.
I can lift the grey wash like a mist,
and the whole flock comes out of hiding.
The goatherd's by that rock, a young lad
with a sweet face. I'll uncover him soon.

Believe me, I had to hide them. Nothing
that lived and breathed, no man, no animal,
could be shown in art. The young zealots
blazed through galleries, slashing, burning,
wherever they saw a face. So I went first,
with my false colours, blending a man
into a wall, a woman into the chair
where she sat, animals into pasture.

When they came, I had a gallery of landscapes
and still lifes. The boy soldiers eyed them,
rifle-butts twitching, but they never saw
what I could see, the flesh in those gaps.
How they didn't suspect such vast stretches
of grass or carpet... Of course they knew nothing
of art. Yet I smiled when one lad said
"They're not ungodly... but they're a bit dull."

Oh indeed, my dear, what could be duller
than a world without you and me, I nearly said,
but bit it back. Well, they're gone now,
the hard cases, the hero-worshippers,
the pure in heart, the mercenaries,
and one dead soldier's face looks as gentle
as another. *You'd have buried me in stone,*
if you'd guessed, but I still mourn you.

And now the godly are fallen, it's safe
for everyone to come out, all the faces,
the limbs. I hid them so well, sometimes,
I'm at a loss to find them. It needs care,
a hesitant touch in each likely place,
much disappointment. But that sudden flutter
of the heart, when a living face
lights up, when an eye meets mine...

The Fuchsia

The great bush by the wall
is a cage of white bones.

When first the house stood empty,
walls lately whitewashed,

you would have said it was waiting
for its owners to come back.

But the old man died, and his widow
sold up the croft. Each year

the walls darken. The gate has rusted
shut since last summer.

A yellowed net still hangs
at what I know was the kitchen window,

but just above, a gap
has opened in the roof-slates,

and the fingers of wind and snow
will be in the loft

where the old man kept
his childhood relics, a painted shield,

a wooden sword. The rain
will crumble and flake them,

like the beams in the ceiling
above the black hearth,

the box bed in the wall
where the old man was born.

Twenty years back, the fuchsia
reached a man's height, heavy

with red, its flowers drenching
the ground like blood.

I don't recall how it bleached
to this bare skeleton,

nor how the face I have seen
framed in red flowers,

staring from a photograph, came
to be mine.

The Bereavement of the Lion-Keeper

for Sheraq Omar

Who stayed, long after his pay stopped,
in the zoo with no visitors,
just keepers and captives, moth-eaten,
growing old together.

Who begged for meat in the market-place
as times grew hungrier,
and cut it up small to feed him,
since his teeth were gone.

Who could stroke his head, who knew
how it felt to plunge fingers
into rough glowing fur, who has heard
the deepest purr in the world.

Who curled close to him, wrapped in his warmth,
his pungent scent, as the bombs fell,
who has seen him asleep so often,
but never like this.

Who knew that elderly lions
were not immortal, that it was bound
to happen, that he died peacefully,
in the course of nature,

but who knows no way to let go
of love, to walk out of sunlight,
to be an old man in a city
without a lion.

Golden Rabbits

He came up for the peace, the scenery,
the stepping back in time, but mostly
because someone told him the rabbits here
were golden. At the time, he'd never
seen rabbits, and if he had, in truth,
they'd have been psychedelic, the stuff
he was on. But somehow the vision
stuck long enough to get him on a train,

a ferry, a bus, out to the far end
of a peninsula. The crofters were kind,
but they all laid bets he wouldn't last.
Around that time, a lot of folk lost
in the twentieth century took this road,
looking for peace, the truth, themselves, God.
Whatever they'd mislaid, the first storm
saw them give up on it and head for home.

But he's still here, after so long, growing
enough to get by, writing a bit, doing
small driving jobs. "You can't eat scenery,"
someone said, but he can, very nearly.
The red rocks nightly catching fire,
a pod of whales, the odd meteor shower,
are what sustains him, like the peat stack
in his shed, or the big winter sack

of tatties. Most of the rabbits are brown,
same as anywhere, but just the odd one
isn't. His only road blocked by snow
each new year, he scrapes ice from his window
and watches them edge close to his scatterings
of crusts, carrot tops, potato peelings,
his heart stopping when, against the white,
one shape glows like clear honey in sunlight.

The Windfarm Angels

I'll never forget my first sighting:
one alone, on a distant hill
– they prefer hills. There was no wind
that day, none at all, and it stood
quite still. Its top arm, pointing
at the sky, blended into its body:
it was just this tall streak of white.
The two other arms stretched out
left and right, like the statue of Christ
in Rio harbour. That was how I knew
it was an angel. That, and the calm
that came off it. It didn't speak
or make a move: it just *was*,
intensely, and I felt better for it,
which is what they do, right?

After that, I looked out for them,
that sudden grace on the skyline,
whenever there seemed no point
in anything. One windy day, watching
a group of three, I realised they were talking,
not just in gesture language, but a murmur,
low, on one note. I couldn't tell
if they meant it only for each other
or for me too. I heard it in my head
long after. I'd switch off from chat,
traffic, muzak, and it was there.

I've noticed, lately, they don't talk
so loud. Even watching a whole flock,
I have to strain to hear. Folk complained
– would you believe – about the noise,
so now they whisper. And some people
want them gone. I couldn't face that,
not now. I've got used to that presence,
that white embrace, being there
when I need it. I know all their haunts.
To think I might climb those hills one day
and find them empty. Jesus.

Pride

He wears his age well, they say:
it's the silver hair, the straight back,

the fifty-year marriage, even.
But it isn't. The pride

inscribed in his eyes, his voice,
his quiet, private smile,

was burned into him decades back
by a kiss in a tent.

Close up, the glacier was fissured,
black with the dusty scribble

of hail and wind, but distance
perfected its whiteness. He lay

in the summer night of the north,
a blue half-dark

of whispered courtship, and fell
asleep on the numbed arm

of love. And next day,
love was frantic, scrabbling for paper

to write it all down. It was read to him,
softly; the others weren't looking,

and he wondered why the poem
was saying goodbye. One night?

He was at an age when the tune,
the summer, the fairground ride,

are always better repeated.
The secret, warm memory

of kisses could not console him
for the absence of kisses.

He thinks differently now. So far
from that time, he can see the problem:

he *was* sixteen, and the man
was the English master... And anyway,

the poem still shines, an ice-field
of unblemished love no weather

or time can write on, a landmark
of its century. Now, in his eighties,

he speaks it from memory, marvelling.
That was me? But it was. The knowledge

superb in his eyes, that hold
no more self-doubt than a hawk's.

Baliasta Kirkyard

1

In a windy kirkyard
between the Atlantic and the North Sea,
among Craigs, Johnstons, Abernethys,
a palm tree and a wave of sand
figure on the stone his grieving workmates
raised to the oilman Rachid Khalifa.

2

Eight crosses, four names: Kristoffer Luthentun,
captain, Peder Silseth, Alfred Stenseth,
and Finn Jensen, who wanted two months
to his twentieth birthday. The ship went down
with seventeen. Since no-one knows
which three washed up nameless on Fetlar,
which three at Easting, which one at Lunna
and which four here, each under a blank cross,
the wall plaque names them all, not leaving out
the two who, in the wreck of a black night,
never left that clashing void, whose bruised bodies
never made land to feel hands' tenderness.

3

Though you lived so close, you do not lie
in this or any kirkyard.

You who had gone no further
than peat hill, pasture, market,

they took you to court three islands away
by cart and ferry and cart and ferry and cart

– and the mare walking alongside.
She'd catch sight of you sometimes, call

in her soft, uncomprehending voice:
you dared not look at her.

Enough loathing already
in your guards' eyes, their insults,

their spit on your face. You still felt
human, a man like them,

but when you and she were burned
they scattered your ashes

on the wind, unwilling any scrap
of you should find rest,

a home, a name on a stone
in Baliasta or anywhere

Best Jesus in Show

See, these country shows, there's always classes
with maybe just one entry. *Six Jam Tarts*
Baked by a Gentleman, or *Female Goat*
Not in Milk. Well, the Jesus van
was like that. Every year, this Malcolm
shows up, in a camper with JESUS SAVES
on the side, parks by the tractors
and waits for people to come and pray.

Only this year, there's another one,
Society for Christian Somethingorother,
facing Malcolm across the show field.
Competition! And we're wondering how
to judge them. With sheep or needlework
or vegetables, there's criteria:
so many marks for size, presentation,
lack of blemishes... But then with tups
or turnips, you know how they're meant to look.

All we had to go on was Malcolm,
who's the hairy sort with sandals,
and this other bloke, who's a suit
and probably works in a call centre.
They're no more alike than a Limousin
and a Friesian, but somehow one of them
has to end up as Best Jesus in Show,
with the other as reserve champion.

Watching the folk group, someone suggested
banjos at noon. Duelling Jesuses?
Give them each five buns and some crackling
from the pig roast, and see which can feed
five thousand? The log-sawing contest
seemed possible, but they didn't fancy
raising a hand and telling the logs to part.

You couldn't use audience figures: no one
went near either of them. In the end
we didn't feel sure enough. Anyway,
there was only one spare rosette
in the committee tent, and the girls
nabbed that, wrote *Prettiest Policeman in Show*
on the ribbon, and gave it to the traffic plod
by the main gate.

The Grave of the Grande Armée at Vilnius

He must have been young indeed,
when he left his home in France,
or Poland, or Portugal,

to follow the Grande Armée.
Maybe he played a drum,
laughed up at the bearded faces,

kept time as they sang their way
over half a continent.
Only free men are men.

At Vilnius-on-two-rivers
they gathered, as summer came on,
and when the emperor said,

"Moscow in twenty days,"
maybe he cheered with the rest.
The sun rang, hammer on metal,

and they sang *Our Fan likes a drink,*
and the country sucked them in.
Week after week, they marched

into empty villages, fields
bare of crops, no one to fight,
only, around their edges,

Kazakhs, the shadows of wolves,
swerving in, snapping, retreating.
The army started to fray,

slipping off, but he was still there,
singing *All the kings must weep,*
when they came to Borodino.

He did not die on the field,
where the fifty thousand were left
to stiffen in autumn frost.

He was with the Grande Armée
entering Moscow, the streets
uncanny and silent. Maybe

he saw a bit of the city,
before its hidden people
set it alight and ran.

Maybe he saw the emperor
ride past that wall of fire
that lit the tears on his face.

Maybe they did still sing
When all the tyrants are dead,
as they tramped the road they had come,

past the dead of Borodino,
past blackened house and field.
November, the first snow fell,

and they huddled close at night,
listening to the wolves.
They started to dream of food.

Fan was baptised in wine,
he'd sing, the rusty taste
of horse-blood still in his mouth.

They could not cling close enough
to keep out the frost; maybe
he lost an ear or a finger,

but he crossed the crazy pontoon
at the Beresina River.
A hundred were swept away,

but when the last of the army
lay starving outside Vilnius,
he was still there, still singing

We're all from the same country,
as the emperor slipped off for France.
Maybe he watched him go.

One grave for the bones of young men
from every land in Europe.
He had no wound: his body,

aching for warmth, was curled
the way, fifteen years before,
it had lain in his mother.

Adzio's Story

Adzio on the beach; he's eleven,
like the century, on holiday,

and the Adriatic is that blue he'll recall,
but never see again. He arches

like a cat, to make the sun stroke him,
warm, content. If he sees, for a moment,

on the edge of his vision, the old man
watching him again, it casts no shadow;

might just rate a mention in the diary,
if nothing more interesting turns up.

When he's grown, when he's Baron Moes
and no-one calls him Adzio any more,

he'll read the book, see the golden boy
and the dark, arm in arm, and know

– how slowly? – *It's me... me and Jasio.*
How will it feel, to watch himself played

like a chess piece, altered to fit
the story? *I wasn't fourteen,*

and why has he made me anaemic?
Looking back, he will think he recalls

eyes bright with hunger. *Only thirty-six?*
He seemed so old... The story shapes itself

to a new shoreline. *Did I fight Jasio?*
The horizon where what was real

shades into fancy is so far off,
so blurred, he can't make it out.

He will never come forward while the writer
still lives, never say *That was me*

you wrote about. The old man smiled to think
the boy would die young... It seems tactless

to stand, middle-aged, where the memory
of *him* should be. Adzio grew up,

but the boy with the honey-coloured hair
and the grey eyes has never left Venice;

still stands between sea and land, looking back
at the real, beckoning into the story.

The Anderson Graveyard, Aith

Two walled gardens, two gates, as if death
had a tradesmen's entrance. One is full
of Taits, Johnstons, Nicolsons, all
this country's names. The salt air of Aith
abrades their histories: hard to make out
the words, where lichen's scabbed over each cut.

Behind the second gate, a chosen garden.
Four stone Celtic crosses, head-high,
ornately carved, facing out to sea.
They have suffered the wind and the lichen
like their poor neighbours: three are grown dim,
but the fourth still reads clear, the name

Robina Anderson, daughter of Janet
and James, widow of William Fraser.
I can trace others now, knowing her:
there's *James*, that's *William*, lost in his boat
off Vementry. The last, not a word
except *of James*, and maybe *beloved*.

Robina's cross shelters behind a tree,
a rare sight here; perhaps it's kept her safe
these ninety years and more, preserved her life
enough to read. She was just forty-three,
had only lately raised her husband's cross,
erected by his loving wife. I'd guess,

among the words the salt has scratched away
from James' and Janet's, there was once mention
of a *loving daughter*. I think this woman
hated the thought of death. She does not say,
on William's cross, that he is just asleep,
nor that they'll meet in heaven: no such hope.

Goodbye, my dear. No more. It means he's gone
for good, unless he leaves something behind
where he lived, something to feel sun and wind,
even if it's his name cut in stone.
There is no word, on his cross or on hers,
of children: no *loving sons* or *daughters*

claim her memorial. Perhaps she made
provision, chose the plain words in advance,
not trusting others with her only chance
of staying here, of not being dead
in name as well as body. It is bright
today, Robina, the whole harbour lit

with deep reflections, boats, hillsides, clouds,
all fixed in glass. George Herbert mourned a day
as calm and still. It's easy to see why
you need to stay; who could walk the roads
of heaven, still missing this? All you could do
was leave your name. Well, if it comforts you,

it worked. When I recall those graveyards,
there are names, trades, ages, but none go
together, except yours, and even now
I can see your cross, your life in brief words,
the names of those you loved. You wanted this
enough, and so it happened. Don't rest in peace,

if peace means nothingness and forgetting
all you once loved: don't come to terms with death,
when all you still want is here in Aith.
Until your stone rubs blank, go on writing
your name in passing eyes. Be here, uneasy,
insistent, the sting in the fine spray.

The Man On His Back

I was waiting for the bus: he walked by
from behind, a man with a man

on his back, a life-size hardboard cut-out
that bowed him down. He bore it

face forward – I suppose there *was* a face,
staring over his head, but I saw only

the back, not destined for display, unpainted,
featureless. He stumbled under its weight

now and then; a man steadied him,
a woman wiped sweat from his forehead.

The walk down Westgate must have seemed long,
seeing nobody, maybe risking

the odd glance up, till the ache in his neck
forced his eyes back to the pavement.

Parents, carers, workers all passed
unburdened, walking free in the sun,

while he carried his private patch
of shadow, the man on his back.

Fiction

Camp 60, Orkney, 1945

It isn't a prison camp, if we plant flowers,
and this can't be the far north,
or why would we bring tables and chairs
outside, to dine alfresco? Our theatre
has proper scenery.

And this isn't a Nissen hut; do you see
corrugated iron anywhere? The brickwork
and the carved stone are only plasterboard
if you touch them. Take them with the eye;
believe what you see.

Chiocchetti is brilliant at painting shadows.
Look at the stone pillars, the gilded beams
of the vault; you can see they're solid.
If your fingers tell you different, will it change
what your eyes know?

Things become more than themselves.
Shipwreck wood is a tabernacle, scrap-iron
a rood screen. Those light-holders, hanging
from chains of silver stars, were beaten
out of tin cans.

Palumbo and Primavera shaped scrap
into candelabra; the white altar
is Bruttapasta's concrete, like the façade
with its belfry and pinnacles. You'd say
it was all marble,

because it seems a place where marble
should be, and sometimes what seems
is what is real. The font is concrete too,
but it looks like stone. Chiocchetti
is painting it

to seem weathered. I said, *Domenico,*
who gets christened, in a prison camp?
He didn't answer. The war is over,
we're all going home soon,
but he has asked

to stay, to finish work on a font
that isn't needed, in a chapel
whose congregation has left. It's gone
beyond him; you can see he's become
part of its story.

He worries about what will happen
to his creation, his face as haunted
as Pennisi's clay Christ above the door.
All we needed was a Nissen hut,
somewhere to call

a chapel. Our theatre has real scenery,
but nothing to match the gold curtains
of our vestry, that open for a man
of earth to step through, transfigured
into a priest.

Googlisms

(Googlism is a web site that throws up definitions and contexts of a search term from web sites trawled by the search engine Google. These 'found poems' are all culled, but otherwise unaltered, from googlisms – the search term in each case is the title.)

1. The Sonnet

the sonnet is a fourteen line poem written in iambic
                                    pentameter
the sonnet is a meditation on mortality
the sonnet is love; usually they are written from a male
                                     perspective
the sonnet is full of such paradoxes
the sonnet is written in iambic pentameter with a few
                               exceptions for emphasis
the sonnet is a lyrical as well as a rhetorical form
the sonnet is a tool of warmonging capitalist masters
the sonnet is a crown

the sonnet is divided into two sections
the sonnet is printed below on the left
the sonnet is like the legendary camel which
the sonnet is running backside cache at 250mhz
the sonnet is a reminder of all those who feel this way
the sonnet is for
the sonnet is slightly too long

the sonnet is not a sonnet anymore?

2. The Poet

the poet is like the prince of the clouds
the poet is the priest of the invisible
the poet is a little god translated from the spanish by
                                        jorge garcía
the poet is $200 per half day

the poet is due to have another book published in
                                        march of 2000
the poet is a creative writing text for students learning
                                        to write poetry
the poet is available as a paperback now and as an audiobook
the poet is evidently preaching to himself the lesson
                                        of fortitude and hope

the poet is trying to say
the poet is simply doing three things at the same time
the poet is unlikely to visit every class in one day
the poet is best taken in moderation

the poet is the voice of the people
the poet is that mouth
the poet is proving that he is a poet
the poet is mistaken for cinna

the poet is always searching for new faces and looks
the poet is about to offer a statement of doctrines
the poet is intrinsically linked with the magic and
                                        language of the poem
the poet is happy she shares a name with a gifted chimp

the poet is rather an old book
the poet is missing
the poet is a liar
the poet is you

3. The Reader

the reader is connected
the reader is powered and in use

the reader is the narrator
the reader is a static object and books come to him to be read

the reader is the central character
the reader is the adversary

the reader is addressed as the writer's equal
the reader is told how

the reader is distracted by
the reader is encouraged to do the exercises

the reader is persuaded to agree by force
the reader is warned

the reader is in control
the reader is in control?

The Street of Small Houses

Wooden booths, just big enough for one,
leaned close on a street stifled

with caraway, saffron, aniseed.
The old men pattered out on their errands

for food and firewood in the peppery air,
sneezing. They were foreigners, clerks

to the spice merchants, settled
among strangers who slowly turned

into neighbours. They went shopping
for small amounts. The city forbade them

marriage: they might live
and trade, but leave no mark.

On the Street of Small Houses
windows were paned

with horn or skin: scant outlook
for the old bachelors.

They got handy about the house,
used to long silences,

fond of their own company. They grew
apart from each other, lost their language

for one in which they would never
take vows or christen children.

They aged into habits, teased by the songs
of boys. Their walks grew shorter

and they passed fewer men they knew
to nod to in the street where ginger

had lost its bite. They drew their houses
round them like dressing-gowns.

Generosity

i.m. John R. Cash

When I heard the slow disease
shake your notes, the tremolo
growing in your voice,

I thought back to how,
once, you sang a duet
on some TV chat show

with an old mate
whose voice was a ghost,
wrecked by tequila. Yet,

though its strength was lost,
the sweetness came over,
because you cut most

of the raw power
from your own, sang scarcely
above a murmur,

deferring tenderly
at every turn.
You'd think there might be

recompense; that even
illness and death might hanker
to match a gentleman
in such a gesture.

Buying Vinyl

I was asking Cal about floor coverings
– I knew it was Cal because his cardboard badge

said CAL in black felt-tip. What I needed
was six metres of wood-effect vinyl

on a roll, and a good reason to fix
Cal's eyes with mine for a few moments

while I told him about it. They were brown,
far darker than the vinyl, forest-pool-effect.

I showed him what I wanted, and he nodded
and said "yes, right away" and spread

the stuff out on the floor and knelt down.
The back of his neck looked as untouched

as new snow. He glanced up under his eyebrows,
shy, and said, "Do me a favour,

hold this still?" So I did, kneeling
beside him at the edge, pressing my hand

where his had been, while he laid
his long steel rule close to the roll

and cut. Clean, straight, beautiful.
I said, "You're good at that" and he smiled,

and I thought, *You can't be more than seventeen.*
He rolled it tight, not easy, the tip

of his tongue just showing, and I wanted
to help, but he hadn't asked, and I was meant

to be the customer, after all.
I'm three times your age. And he mastered it.

All tied up firmly. I was proud of him.
He puzzled for a moment, licked

the end of his biro, then wrote the bill.
"You pay them over there." It was good value,

I thought, as I checked the VAT,
and he hadn't even charged for the smile.

In Love Without

Being *in love with* would be easy,
together in that place where no path
leads where it ought, in that curious light
where perspective goes all to hell.
The two moons, the Escher staircases,
the clueless maze, they'd be pure adventure
if they were mirrored in your eyes
and his; if he were there with you.

But you're in love without, seeing aslant
what he sees straight, lost on the roads
that take him home. It's another country
in the same space, in no eyes but yours.
Close by, far off, he laughs; waves a hand
past your face. "What planet are you on?"

The Thief of Love

I will come like a thief if I have to,
soft-footed. I won't force an entry,
just find one,

some sash with a gap. I'll slip
a fingertip in, ease it open
while you're asleep.

You'll be out when I feel your cool sheets
on my skin, when I stroll through your rooms
handling, enjoying.

I'll access your email, your passwords,
click on your history, trace you
through cyberspace.

Did you think I would come to the door
as honest folk do; play fair?
Love has no pride,

no honour; it takes what it's given
and what it can get. It begs
without shame; why not this?

And I am each chancer, levanter
and picklock who gives his heart freely
to what's out of reach,

far above, safely owned, and schemes how
to coax it to hand, one way
or another.

Love Is

Each time you go out, I wonder
if you'll meet them, the ones
warped beyond help,

bored enough to break
what can be broken:
benches, saplings, bones.

Love is knowing they're out there
even when they aren't.

I see their smiles
as they call you. I see
your face, open,

trusting, as they take you
to some unwatched place.
I see your eyes

widen as they turn
on you, and I think
they laugh, then,

at your pain, but still more
at your surprise; how easy
it was to fool you.

Love is dreaming things they could do
that even they don't guess.

Up to the moment
when you walk through the door
whole, smiling, safe,

you are lying in the dark
I made in my head,
and their grins are fixed

where my blade etched them.
Your name, which they never
cared to ask,

I burn carefully,
with a flourish of pokerwork,
into their flesh.

Love is knowing I could do
anything they could.

Ballad of the Lovesick Traveller

You roll a rizla, and your friends
half-heartedly protest,
but she, ex-smoker that she is,
lights it and holds your wrist.
We fan the acrid smoke away;
she tastes it in your kiss.
And what is that but love, my dear,
when nothing tastes amiss?

She's twenty-five; she wants to dance
and feel the pulsing sound.
You're fifty-four; you smile and shrug
and let her take your hand.
On each young face you read the words
No fool like an old fool.
And what is that but love, my dear,
that doesn't mind at all?

She counts the days like miracles
since all the world was new.
You see your image in her eyes
and can't believe it's you.
We, on the edge of all that light,
feel opened, warmed, alive.
And what is that but love, my dear,
that has so much to give?

You crossed the world to see old friends,
not thinking any harm.
Now all your journeys lead elsewhere
and nothing is the same.
And in your home of thirty years,
the one whose trust you have
expects you like tomorrow's post.
And what is that but love?

Murderers Grow Old

Murderers grow old in a California prison
carefully designed for wheelchair access.

Down wide corridors, gripping the handrails,
stopping for hits of Ventolin, the lifers

walk stiffly to the visitors' windows,
with their hearing loops, to the library

full of large-print books and audiotapes,
to the clinic, its white walls papered

with diabetic diet-sheets. The guards
who take frail arms, stop feet from stumbling,

stroke crumbs off a cheek that might be
their father's, know what each one was.

The gunman with the Parkinson's tremor,
the heroin boss who cries when he injects

his insulin, the hooked arthritic hands
that have strangled children. Murderers grow old

dozing on benches, under the sun that shines
on parks and prison exercise yards,

and maybe their dreams are tormented
with many deaths, or maybe just the one

that haunts old men in parks, innocent
of any crime, serving the same sentence.

The Garden of the Last Nizam

In the garden of the last Nizam
bare, unpruned rose branches straggle

to a single bud. The fountain is choked
with leaves. Weeds force apart

the wall's cracks, overgrow the paths
that are going back. No-one walks here

any more. The old man has forgotten
what once he cared for: the tame fish

he liked to feed, the fruit warmed
by sunlight, the scent of flowers

at dusk, the rusting carts, laden
with rubies that glow through brambles.

The Ex-Poet Writes HTML

He types "go here"; encloses it
in an anchor ref. Now, if you click
on the words,

the thing will happen. He writes code
to make words dance, change colour,
come alive.

He can make them shape the image
of his new book cover,
with secret text

embedded; when the cursor rests,
adventure leaps out.
And he can't believe

the power, the way words move,
at last, as he wants,
the way they turn

into sounds and patterns, the way
they send his readers
on the journey

he chose for them. He spends
whole days online, can't sleep
for thinking up

page after page, hooked
on creation, and he hasn't written
a poem in months.

Flying Into Sunset

He's flying late, above dense cloud,
close-coiled rope on a ship's deck,

toward the core of all redness
bleeding rose, wine, molten copper

over the blue-white ice-field, and nobody
watching below the cloud, he knows,

ever saw these colours. They'll be going
home now, the earthbound,

escaping from work. Little clumps
of pink cumulus like tumbleweed

blow across the flight path. And they pay him
to do this, to be here, though he knows

he'd pay them. And when the blaze
narrows to a red line, goes out,

all the matches at once, it leaves no dark,
not up here, just uncanny blue,

perpetual day, a story
with no last line, a childhood

out of time. *No-one saw where
the bird went, but some said it flew*

straight into the sun. In the ice-field
polynyas open: he can see the dark,

ocean-deep, below him, trembling
with threaded points of light,

and it's Birmingham, but he doesn't need
to know that yet.

Place Names

There was a valley with a peat burn;
it sloped down to a shelving bay
between two headlands. Southward, a smooth hump,
northward, a long thin cliff that broke
the water. The current flowed strong, brought in
branches and wrack. The land was stony,
where it wasn't bog. Along the rocks
of an inlet to the north, seals basked.

The people came for fresh water, for driftwood,
for the harbour sheltered by Whale Ness
and the Arm. Helgi, Arne, Grim
picked rocks, one by one, from Staney Rig
and built their walls. They dug trenches
through the bright poisonous green of Marshfield.
Fishing was good: now and then rich meat
and fat from a kill in Seli Geo.

They happened to the land: it happened
to them. In the drained field
horses grazed; the farmer at Arnastead
tried pig-keeping. The seals became shy
and left their inlet. A Dutch ship went down
and the current brought six bodies
into Woodwick. The farmers buried them
on Whale Ness and shared out the cargo.

No landlord forced them out of the valley
in the end. The last farmer's son
at Grimsetter left for the oil rigs;
the widow at Swinister moved to town.
What the land gave them, they no longer needed:
Hrossafield, its trenches flower-choked,
is going back to marsh, and no-one tends
the graves on Hollanders Ness.

Following the stream down Burnadale
will bring you to the ruined croft township
of Woodwick. The bay itself is sheltered,
a good picnic spot. On Hollanders Ness
may be seen the graves of six sailors
from a Dutch wreck, and Hrossafield bog, in June,
glows red with marsh-orchids. At the inlet
of Seli Geo, watch out for seals.

Nicola's Tree

i.m. Nicola Samuel, who was my student from 1995-6

They planted your tree: it's small
and frail, like you.

But it stands rooted, and you weren't
at all. Always on the move,

if a bit breathless. Bright,
sudden, vehemently alive.

Little finch, little fall of water
chattering on rock, quick glint

of sunlight, what tree
could be you? They'd need make

the leaves of mercury.
Spun-glass stem, slender candle,

wood will never well
with light like your skin.

Briefer than any tree,
sweet moment, a breath

of air lives for ever
if it shapes the right song.

Learning Hindi

I rolled an incorrect *r*
and my life took a new peacock.

Words misprint as worlds
all the time. I woke

with a new voice, raucous
and haunting. Though I walked

in the old way, eyes
bent on the ground, my humility

was only manners.
In my mind there hid,

folded, the northern lights,
a curtain waterfall

of colours, trembling
like jewels on thin wire.

Almost blue, almost green, almost purple,
too iridescent

to pin down, vibrations
in the air, eye-music.

I can hear the notes, unplayed,
I don't need to open

the great, rustling sheaf.
So heavy, so secret,

what I am. Only
my cry, shaking,

ragged with delight,
gives me away.

The Curious Drawer

*How then can the curious drawer watch, and as it were
catch those lovely graces, witty smilings and those
stolen glances which suddenly like lightning pass,
and another countenance taketh place?*
        — Nicholas Hilliard, *The Arte of Limning*

1.The Ermine

*And with a pretty little tooth of some ferret or
stoat or other wild little beast you may burnish
your gold and silver.*

She is almost lost in points of light.
Her gown the dark ground, sown

with gold and silver, stiff with jewels,
her ruff a radiance, as if

her face shed moonlight. I have made
filigree of her hair. On her left sleeve,

through intricate patterns, crevasses
of velvet, a small wild creature

climbs like a pet. You may see,
if you will, majesty

in the tiny crown it wears, virginity
in the startling white I ground

on jasper and mixed in a clean shell.
I see suddenness, unsuspected

ivory daggers, a swift savagery
that takes the breath away.

2. Young Man Among Roses

Know also that parchment is the only good and
best thing to limn on, but it must be virgin
parchment, such as never bore hair, but young
things found in the dam's belly.

I lean him against my wall,
which I will turn
into an oak,

his head inclining
to its rough bark
as if he listened

to some friend. Too slender
his long legs, like some deer
or colt half-grown.

I hang his cloak
off one shoulder,
feigning negligence,

lay his right hand
above his heart,
as who should say

"I am in love",
then I make roses
grow all around him,

pattern the ground
of his white hose
with their airy stems.

On the black cloak
pale buds, picked out
like pearls. Roses arch

over him, curve him
to the trunk where his sorrows
would like to seek

shelter, where he would curl,
if it were hollow,
rocking in the dark.

3. Sidney's Sister

The best black is velvet black, which is ivory
burnt in a crucible.

Is it not strange that bone
should burn black?

Ashes sealed from the air
in salted clay,

fired red-hot, then cooled,
softened with water,

drop by drop, for her gown.
Within a perfect circle

I nest circles, white ruff
on black velvet,

red curls against a sky
of ultramarine, jet beads

clasping a white throat
close. Circles of lace,

hair, stone, drawing the gaze
inward to the stillness

at the heart
of all the circles,

her frozen face,
her bereaved eyes.

4. Henry Percy, 9th Earl of Northumberland

I would wish anybody to be well resolved with
themselves beforehand with what grace they would
stand, and seem as though they never had resolved.

Pansies and violets, petals
bruised and soaked, gave me green,

the lawn he lay on
in his black suit. Some scholar

or divine he seemed
among the flowers, even

with that wave of lace breaking
at collar and cuff.

His hair, brown-gold, combed back
softly, his cheek resting

on one white hand, his body
stretched out at ease.

The book, pink-tasselled,
forgotten at his elbow,

fallen open at love poems
perhaps, or the holy psalms,

anywhere but the history
of his rebel kin,

plotters, traitors, kingmakers
whose blood bloomed

on the scaffold, in the Tower
and across the fields

of Shrewsbury, Towton, Bramham Moor,
drenching the grass.

5. Unknown Young Man Against
a Background of Flames

Let your apparel be of silk, such as sheddeth
least dust or hairs.

My sitters come dressed in their finest: it is I
who must stand bare-headed before them
in a plain white shirt. My colours
are fresh-mixed in the shell, water distilled,
gum arabic pure in its ivory box.
On the burnished card where a face will live
for ever, nothing of me must fall,
not a hair nor a fleck of dandruff. I curb
my tongue, for fear of spittle. In cold weather
I breathe behind my hand.

I am skilled in surfaces: the depth of velvet,
the dazzle of lace, the way light wells
from a pearl or scatters off diamond. But here
is undress, flesh glowing
through thin silk, more ardent
than the flames of love, or so
he would have someone think. He fondles
the chain against his bare throat, shows
the ring on his hand: *see, I wear*
your tokens. I burn for you.

This penitent in silk, this martyr
to love. When you hold him
close in his jewelled case, remember
limning is an art of secrets. I look
for a face few have seen. That longing
in his eyes, he was gazing
at his warm cloak, hung
carefully on my wall,
while I opened his thin shirt,
the match of mine.

Acknowledgements

Some of these poems have previously appeared in *Acumen, the Forward Anthology of Poetry 2005, Fulcrum, the Poetry etc web site, PN Review, Poetic Licence, Poetry Review, Poetry Scotland, Poetry Wales, Sampler, Seam, The Bridport Competition Anthology 2003*, the Strokestown Festival web site, *The Literary Review* (USA), *The New Shetlander, The New Welsh Review, The Times Literary Supplement* and *The Yellow Crane*.

Thank you to the Poetry Book Society for choosing this book as one of its Quarterly Recommendations.

www.geocities.com/sheenaghpugh